Cockroaches:

Here, There, and Everywhere

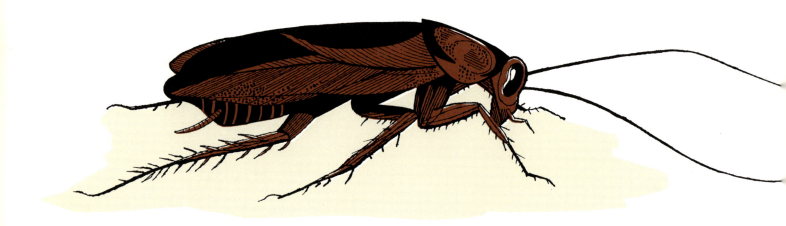

Cockroaches:
HERE, THERE, AND EVERYWHERE

By Laurence Pringle

ILLUSTRATED BY *James and Ruth McCrea*

THOMAS Y. CROWELL COMPANY · NEW YORK

LET'S-READ-AND-FIND-OUT SCIENCE BOOKS

Editors: **DR. ROMA GANS,** Professor Emeritus of Childhood Education, Teachers College, Columbia University

DR. FRANKLYN M. BRANLEY, Chairman and Astronomer of The American Museum–Hayden Planetarium

Air Is All Around You	*Gravity Is a Mystery*	*Seeds by Wind and Water*
Animals in Winter	*Hear Your Heart*	*Shrimps*
A Baby Starts to Grow	*High Sounds, Low Sounds*	*The Skeleton Inside You*
Bees and Beelines	*How a Seed Grows*	*Snow Is Falling*
Before You Were a Baby	*How Many Teeth?*	*Spider Silk*
The Big Dipper	*How You Talk*	*Starfish*
Big Tracks, Little Tracks	*Hummingbirds in the Garden*	*Straight Hair, Curly Hair**
Birds at Night	*Icebergs*	*The Sun: Our Nearest Star*
Birds Eat and Eat and Eat	*In the Night*	*The Sunlit Sea*
Bird Talk	*It's Nesting Time*	*A Tree Is a Plant*
The Blue Whale	*Ladybug, Ladybug, Fly Away Home*	*Upstairs and Downstairs*
The Bottom of the Sea	*The Listening Walk*	*Use Your Brain*
The Clean Brook	*Look at Your Eyes**	*Watch Honeybees with Me*
Cockroaches: Here, There, and Everywhere	*A Map Is a Picture*	*Weight and Weightlessness*
Down Come the Leaves	*The Moon Seems to Change*	*What Happens to a Hamburger*
A Drop of Blood	*My Five Senses*	*What I Like About Toads*
Ducks Don't Get Wet	*My Hands*	*What Makes a Shadow?*
The Emperor Penguins	*My Visit to the Dinosaurs*	*What Makes Day and Night*
Find Out by Touching	*North, South, East, and West*	*What the Moon Is Like**
Fireflies in the Night	*Oxygen Keeps You Alive*	*Where Does Your Garden Grow?*
Flash, Crash, Rumble, and Roll	*Rain and Hail*	*Where the Brook Begins*
Floating and Sinking	*Rockets and Satellites*	*Why Frogs Are Wet*
Follow Your Nose	*Salt*	*The Wonder of Stones*
Glaciers	*Sandpipers*	*Your Skin and Mine**

*AVAILABLE IN SPANISH

Copyright © 1971 by Laurence Pringle. Illustrations copyright © 1971 by James and Ruth McCrea. All rights reserved. Except for use in a review, the reproduction or utilization of this work in any form or by any electronic, mechanical, or other means, now known or hereafter invented, including xerography, photocopying, and recording, and in any information storage and retrieval system is forbidden without the written permission of the publisher. Published simultaneously in Canada by Fitzhenry & Whiteside Limited, Toronto. Manufactured in the United States of America.

L.C. Card 79-132301

ISBN 0-690-19679-2
      0-690-19680-6 (LB)

1   2   3   4   5   6   7   8   9   10

Cockroaches:
Here, There, and Everywhere

Some insects are pests. People don't like them. They swat flies. They slap mosquitoes. They squash cockroaches.

Of all the insects, cockroaches are the ones people dislike most. People try to kill cockroaches when they see them. But cockroaches are tough. They are hard to get rid of. Cockroaches have lived with humans for a million years. When men still lived in caves, cockroaches were right there with them.

The first cockroaches were here on earth long before the first men—even before the first dinosaurs. Fossils of roaches have been found in rocks that were formed 300 million years ago. The first cockroaches we know about looked very much like the ones we see today.

3

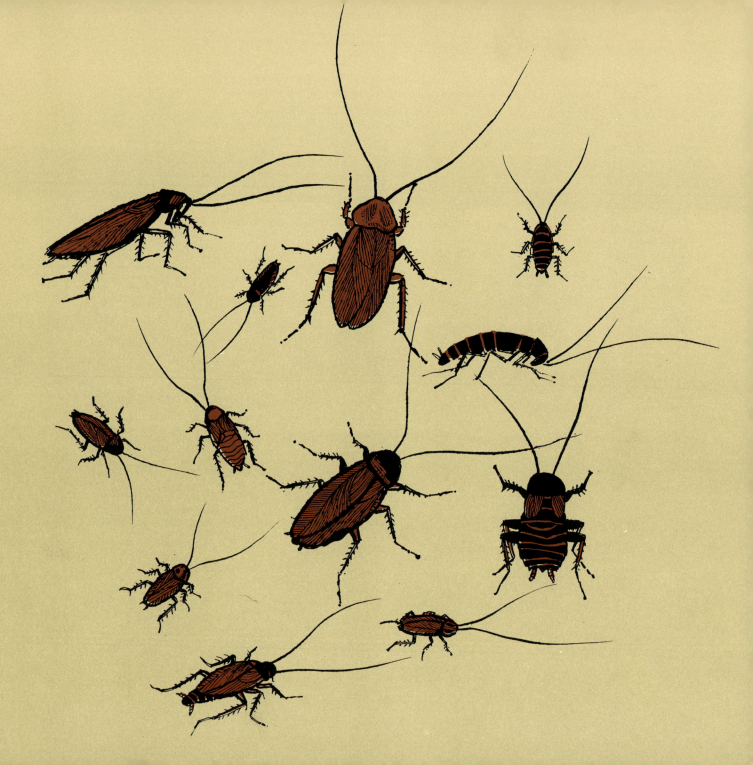

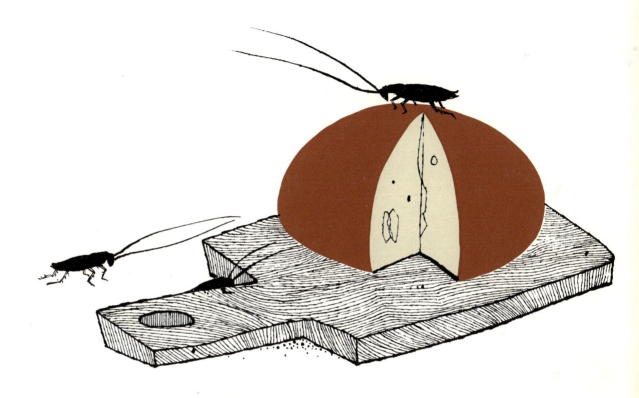

Today there are about 3,500 different kinds of cockroaches in the world. Most of them live outdoors in the tropics where it is warm. Only a few kinds stay indoors with humans.

Cockroaches are found all over the world. They travel from country to country on ships. They go just about everywhere man goes. They live deep in mines and high in skyscrapers. They travel in submarines and airplanes.

Cockroaches have not gone to the moon—yet.

Roaches live where they can keep warm, and can find food. Wherever humans live, bits of food are left around. This is fine for cockroaches.

Cockroaches eat any food they can find. In kitchens they find crumbs and uncovered food. But they also eat garbage. Sometimes they even eat wood, wallpaper, ink, glue, and shoe polish.

Roaches usually hide during the day. They squeeze their flat, slippery bodies into cracks and crannies. Maybe they feel safe when they are in a tight spot.

At night they creep out and search for food and water. Roaches need a lot of water. That is why you often see them in kitchens and bathrooms.

Most roaches have sticky pads between their claws. They can climb straight up glass, tile, wood, or metal.

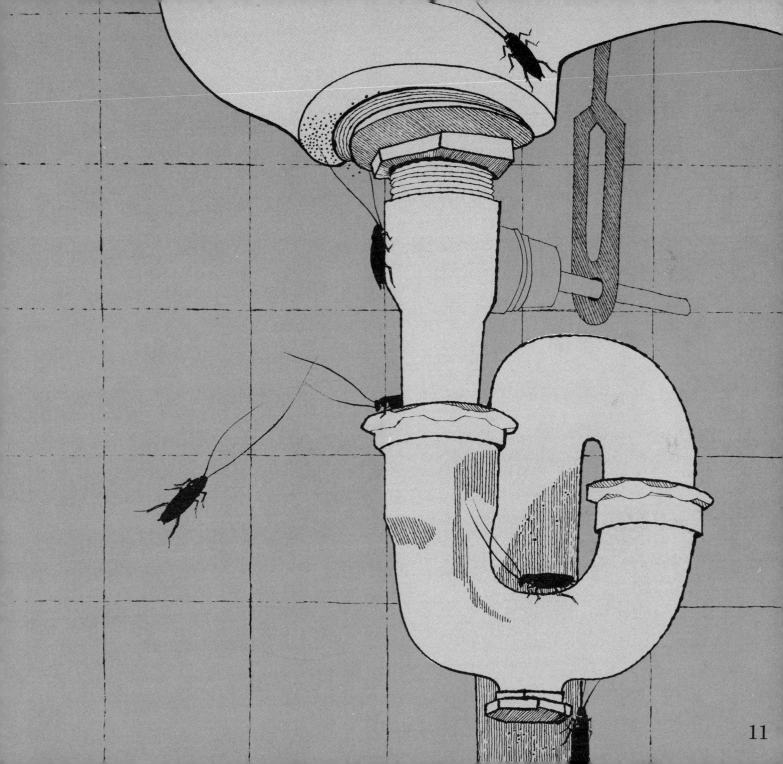

Wherever roaches go, their two long antennae sweep the air ahead. Cockroaches smell and feel with their antennae. The antennae are a great help when a roach has to find its way across a dark room.

It is hard to surprise a roach. Two little tails, called *cerci,* help it to be alert. The cerci are covered with tiny hairs. A sound or a small puff of air is enough to disturb the hairs. This warns the roach of danger.

Suppose you try to step on a cockroach. As your foot comes down, air is pushed ahead of it. The air bends the hairs on the roach's cerci. The hairs are connected to nerves. A message zips from these nerves to other nerves in the roach's legs. The message reaches the leg muscles and the roach starts to run. All this happens in a tiny part of a second.

The roach runs to the nearest hideout. Cockroaches are speedy runners. Most grown-up roaches have wings, but the kinds you find indoors seldom fly. Young ones never have wings.

Cockroaches don't eat much, but they spoil a lot of food with their body wastes. Roaches may carry germs of diseases that affect people. So far they haven't been blamed for causing much sickness. To be safe, though, we shouldn't allow cockroaches near food.

One way to get rid of roaches is to starve them. We do this by not leaving food around. It takes time to starve them, because cockroaches can live a month or more without food. However, if they can't find garbage, or wallpaper, or even shoe polish to eat, they will look for another home.

Some people spray poisons in places where roaches live. Sometimes a poison kills all except a few roaches. These few are not hurt by the poison. We say they are *resistant* to it. When these roaches mate and have young, some of their young are also resistant to the poison. Soon many roaches are around again. The old poison does not bother them. Then a new poison must be developed.

People are trying to find better ways to get rid of roaches. At mating time, cockroaches are attracted to each other by special odors. Scientists are studying what makes these smells. Perhaps the smells can be used to lure cockroaches into traps.

21

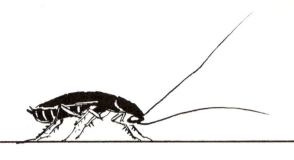

About two weeks after mating, a female roach lays a packet of eggs. Some kinds of roaches just drop the egg pack wherever they are. Others hide it in a safe place. Still others carry the pack until the eggs hatch.

Egg Pack

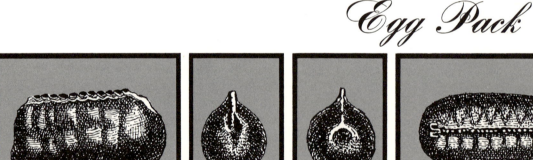

SIDE END END TOP

The egg pack splits open. One or two dozen little roaches wiggle out. Young roaches are called *nymphs*. They are white and have no wings. They scatter and search for food. In a few hours their skins turn dark.

The nymph grows until its skin gets too tight. Then it *molts,* shedding its old skin. The nymph begins to molt by taking air into its body. As the body puffs up with air, the skin splits down the back. The nymph wriggles out. The new skin is soft and white. It soon turns hard and dark. Sometimes a nymph eats its old skin.

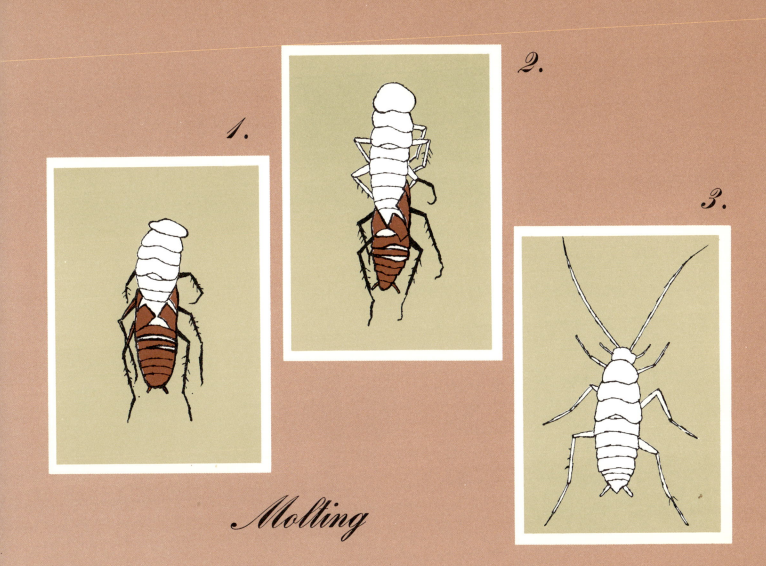

Molting

The nymph gets bigger each time it molts. Its wings begin to appear. After many weeks and many molts, the nymph is almost grown up. Its skin splits once more. A full-grown cockroach squirms out.

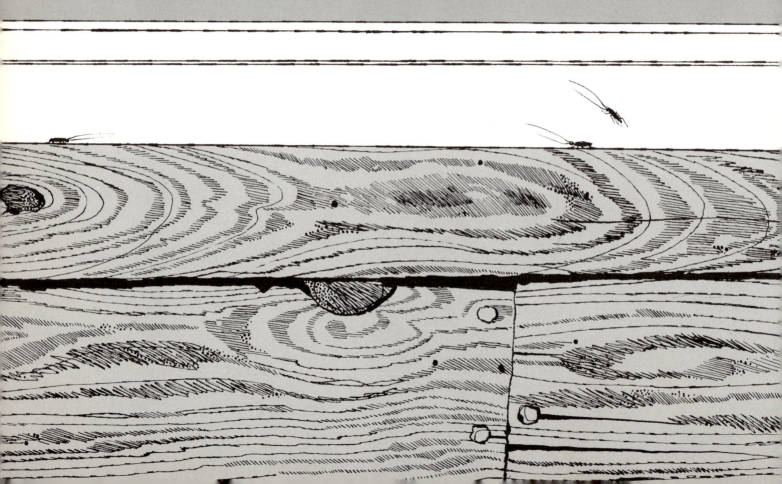

Many nymphs die before they grow up. Sometimes they die of disease. Sometimes spiders hunt and kill them. Another roach killer is the house centipede. It is useful to have around. But the looks of this creepy animal frighten some people.

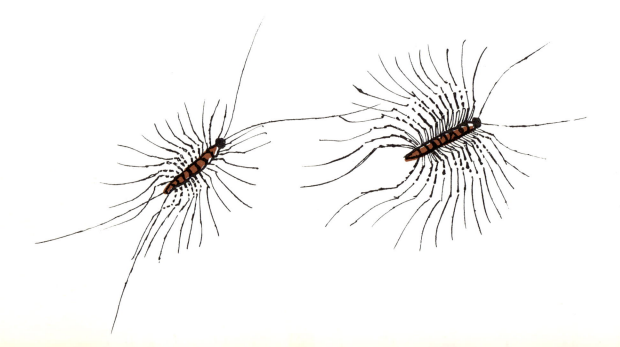

Scientists keep cockroaches on purpose. They study them. They want to know more about how roaches grow. What scientists learn about roaches may help us to understand and control them. It may also help us to understand the lives of other animals.

Scientists have tested cockroaches to see how "smart" they are. Roaches can find their way through a puzzle called a *maze*. Compared with other insects, they are quick learners. This helps them survive in the homes they share with man.

Roaches will probably go on living with people. And people will go on disliking them. But it could be worse. On an island near Africa lives a roach that is almost three inches long. It makes loud hissing noises. Luckily it doesn't live indoors. Aren't you glad it doesn't live with you?

ABOUT THE AUTHOR

Laurence Pringle writes that he is particularly interested in cockroaches because they are so successful: scientists have predicted that roaches will be living on earth long after men have vanished. His research for this book was aided by scholarly publications—and by the testimony of friends who have had firsthand experience with the insects.

Mr. Pringle has degrees in wild life conservation from Cornell and the University of Massachusetts, and has studied forestry and journalism at Syracuse University. He is the author of many books on nature for young people, several of which are illustrated with his own photographs.

ABOUT THE ILLUSTRATORS

Ruth McCrea was born in Jersey City, New Jersey. Her husband is a native of Peoria, Illinois. Since they met in art school, the McCreas have been working together on book design, writing, and illustrating.

James and Ruth McCrea now live in Bayport, Long Island, in a more-than-100-year-old house which they share with one son, two daughters, and innumerable spiders. These spiders caused many a shriek and dash for the fly-swatter when the children were small. However, after reading the manuscript for this book, the McCreas think they may have discovered one reason why they have never seen a cockroach in their dusty old house!